KV-013-521

Wolfgang Amadeus Mozart was born on 27 January 1756 in Salzburg, now in Austria, then part of Bavaria. His birthplace in a street called Getreidegasse, where the family lived until 1773, is now a Mozart museum. He was the last child of seven – the only other to survive into adulthood was his older sister Nannerl, born in 1751. She too was a talented musician, travelling with the family and performing brilliantly on the piano. Mozart's father Leopold was a court musician, composer and violin teacher; in 1756 he published a violin tutor which became famous throughout Europe.

Young Wolfgang Amadeus was a musically talented child, beginning to learn pieces and compose some of his own at the age of five. One of these early compositions, an *Allegro* from 1762 is included here. Proud father Leopold thought nothing of exhibiting his children's talents, taking Wolfgang and Nannerl to Munich in 1762 to perform, and later that year to Passau, Linz and Vienna. Leopold kept travel diaries, detailing his children's successes; the nobleman Count Zinzendorf reported that Mozart 'plays marvellously, he is a child of spirit, lively, charming'. His precocity was also noted in an Augsburg newspaper the following year, which stated that he could 'play in an adult manner, improvise in various styles, accompany at sight, play with a cloth covering the keyboard, add a bass to a given theme, and name any note that was sounded.' A much more ambitious trip to Paris and London followed, stopping en route at many important musical centres including Munich, Augsburg, Mainz, Frankfurt, Aachen and Brussels where the children could perform and Mozart was able to meet other composers. In Paris Mozart's first publications appeared – sonatas for keyboard and violin. The family spent 15 months in London, and played at court for George III. Mozart probably composed his first symphonies at 180 Ebury Street in Chelsea in 1764, commemorated by a plaque on the house. The symphonies composed in London are astonishingly accomplished works for a boy of nine, despite the fact that throughout his childhood Mozart does not seem to have received any formal musical tuition or proper schooling – presumably his father Leopold taught him.

...he could 'play in an adult manner, improvise in various styles, accompany at sight, play with a cloth covering the keyboard, add a bass to a given theme, and name any note that was sounded.'

The family returned to Salzburg laden down with presents from the courts where the children had performed. Between 1766 and 1771, Mozart arranged and composed further works including his first opera *La Finta Semplice*, and his father took the family to Vienna. On 27 October 1769 Mozart was appointed Konzertmeister to the court at Salzburg. In December that year, Leopold and Wolfgang set off for Italy, to show off Wolfgang's talents and also absorb something of the land of opera. Their itinerary is impressive even by modern standards – they visited Innsbruck, Rovereto, Verona, Mantua, Parma, Bologna and Rome where they heard Allegri's haunting *Miserere* in the Sistine Chapel, which Mozart wrote out after a single hearing. Whilst in Rome, Mozart had a papal audience where he was honoured with a knighthood. The journey continued to Naples and Milan. Here, in October 1770, Mozart began work on the opera *Mitridate, rè di Ponto* which was premiered on 26 December. The foundations were laid for further operatic commissions, resulting in further Italian journeys in 1771 and 1772. On 9 July 1772, Mozart was formally employed as Konzertmeister at the Salzburg court, a position which had been honorary until then. In January 1773 he composed *Exsultate, jubilate*, a motet for soprano and small orchestra in three movements, ending with the brilliant Allelujah included here.

The symphonies composed in London are astonishingly accomplished works for a boy of nine...

Further trips to Vienna enabled Mozart to immerse himself in the latest compositions by Haydn, whose string quartets he particularly admired. During 1773-74 he composed further symphonies, his first string quintet, concertos, serenades and masses. He received a commission for an opera for Munich, and began work on *La finta giardiniera* in 1774. Early piano sonatas date from this period, together with the five violin concertos, divertimentos and serenades including the magnificent 'Haffner' serenade K250. This was composed for the wedding of Elisabeth Haffner, daughter of a wealthy Salzburg citizen. The first piano concertos followed, many written for particular patrons or performers.

In 1777, Mozart left the employment of the archbishop in Salzburg and set out – this time with his mother – in search of a better position elsewhere, travelling to Munich, Augsburg and Mannheim. In Mannheim his attempts to secure a position were unsuccessful, but he composed several works for the flautist J.B. Wendling, and fell in love with a young soprano, Aloysia Weber. Urged on by letters from his father, he continued his journey to Paris, where he composed, taught and sought out potential patrons. His mother fell ill and died in Paris on 3 July 1778. A better position as court organist in Salzburg became available, and Mozart returned by January 1779 to take this up. During his long absence, he had the opportunity to absorb the musical styles prevalent in different cities, such as the celebrated 'Mannheim' style. This was developed by composers writing at the Mannheim court, who had a superbly disciplined orchestra at their disposal, able to produce striking dynamic effects with precision. The violin sonata K296, whose slow movement is included here, dates from this period.

In 1780 Mozart received a commission for an opera from Munich, and began work on *Idomeneo*. Premiered in January 1781, this was a great success. The orchestral accompaniment was written with the virtuoso Mannheim orchestra – now resident in Munich – in mind. Returning to Salzburg after *Idomeneo*, Mozart soon left for Vienna where his employer was celebrating the accession of Emperor Joseph II. Here, fresh from his triumphs in Munich, he was treated little better than a servant, and was eventually released from his employment at Salzburg, 'with a kick on my arse, by order of our worthy Prince

Archbishop'. Settled in Vienna, Mozart earned his living by teaching, composing and performing. He took part in an improvisation competition with the composer Muzio Clementi, and embarked upon a relationship with Constanze Weber, sister of Aloysia who had spurned him a few years earlier. He met Haydn in 1781, later dedicating a set of six string quartets to him; their warm friendship is well documented, and Haydn is reported to have said to Leopold Mozart, 'Before God, I tell you that your son is the greatest composer known to me in person or by name. He has taste, and, what is more, the greatest knowledge of composition'.

During 1782 Mozart worked on the opera *Die Entführung aus dem Serail* (*The Abduction from the Harem*), successfully premiered that summer. Its setting on the Turkish coast gave Mozart the opportunity to cater for Viennese tastes by including some lively 'Turkish' music, characterised by short phrases, and exotic orchestration using piccolo and an expanded percussion section. In similar Turkish style, the 'Rondo alla Turca' from the Piano Sonata K331 is included here, together with the Andante grazioso slow movement. Other works from this period include the Haffner Symphony (the Minuet is included in this album), C minor Mass, a wind serenade, piano concertos and the masterly Quintet for piano and wind K452. Mozart and Constanze married on 4 August 1782 in St Stephen's Cathedral, Vienna; he was 25, she was 20. Their first child, Raimund Leopold, was born in June 1783 but died in August that year.

...Haydn is reported to have said to Leopold Mozart, 'Before God, I tell you that your son is the greatest composer known to me in person or by name. He has taste, and, what is more, the greatest knowledge of composition'.

In 1784 Mozart began to keep a list of his new works, *Verzeichnüss aller meiner Werke*, giving the title and the opening musical phrase of each, a catalogue of immense importance to future generations in understanding Mozart's output. On 11 December he became a freemason – an association that was to inform much of his later work. 1785 was a busy time for him; but although he was at his peak of composing and performing, and receiving glowing newspaper reviews for concerts, his finances were dire and he asked his publisher Hoffmeister for a loan. The two magnificent piano quartets in G minor and E flat were written in 1785, and two piano concertos; the slow Andante movement of the C major concerto K467, much loved for its beautiful *cantabile* melody line, is included here. It is often known as 'Elvira Madigan' after a film in which this movement was used.

Mozart's main energies were devoted to collaboration with the celebrated Italian librettist Da Ponte on a new opera, *Le nozze di Figaro* (*The Marriage of Figaro*), which was premiered at the Burgtheater, Vienna on 1 May 1786. In the following years it was performed in several other German cities. The collaboration with Da Ponte was an important one for Mozart, and resulted in three magnificent operas – *Don Giovanni* and *Così fan tutte* followed. In 1787 he travelled to Prague, spending four weeks

there and composing the Prague symphony. There, he was commissioned to write another opera for the following autumn, *Don Giovanni*, also to a libretto by Da Ponte. His father Leopold became ill, and died in May that year. Compositions from this period include chamber works, songs, a piano concerto and *Eine Kleine Nachtmusik* for string orchestra. (The first movement theme, and Romance and Minuetto are included in this album.)

The premiere of *Don Giovanni* was planned for 14 October, but it was postponed until 29 October, Mozart completing the last part just two days before. On his return to Vienna he was appointed to the post of court Kapellmeister, which provided a reasonable salary and carried with it some status, but his financial worries continued, and more begging letters were written. During the summer of 1788, he composed his three last symphonies. The graceful minuet from Symphony no. 39 in E flat and the first movement theme from the G minor Symphony, no. 40, are included here.

In 1789 Mozart travelled with Prince Lichnowsky (later a patron of Beethoven) to Berlin, visiting Prague, Dresden, Leipzig and Potsdam en route, where he was able to play chamber music, improvise, give concerts, and visit the Prussian court. Towards the end of this year he began work on the opera *Così fan tutte*, a further collaboration with Da Ponte. This was premiered on 26 January 1790, but the fee Mozart received seemed to make little difference to his precarious finances. During summer 1791, Mozart composed the beautiful motet *Ave verum corpus* for the choirmaster at Baden, Anton Stoll (included here). He began work on a collaboration with the actor-manager Emanual Schikaneder, to write the opera *Die Zauberflöte* (*The Magic Flute*). At about the same time he received a commission from a stranger who requested Mozart to compose a requiem (in fact the commissioner was a Count who wanted to pass off the composition as his own work). Another operatic commission from Prague was for *La clemenza di Tito* (*The Clemency of Titus*); Mozart conducted the premiere on 6 September. By now his operatic works were receiving acclaim in the many theatres where they were performed. He also wrote the famous clarinet concerto for Anton Stadler.

Illness took over towards the end of 1791. Whilst Mozart slaved away to complete the *Requiem*, he imagined that his own death was near. A few friends gathered around his bed to sing through parts of the unfinished *Requiem*, but he died of severe fever early on 5 December 1791, aged 35.

Despite his early death, Mozart left behind a large body of work, including many compositions that are still considered to be amongst the finest in musical history. He refined the Classical ideals of form and balance to their peak, and his mastery of every genre, from the string quartet to opera, is evident in all the pieces presented here. **Elizabeth Robinson**

Note: Some pieces in this book have been transposed into simpler keys to suit grades 2-4.

Ah Vous Dirai-je, Maman

(K265 Theme & Three Variations)

Composed by Wolfgang Amadeus Mozart

Moderately

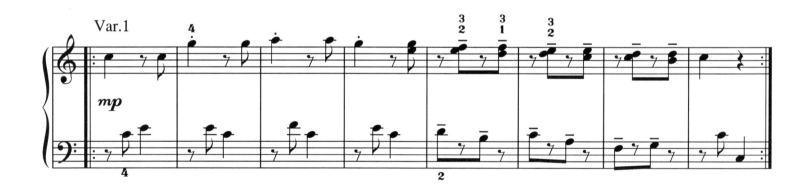

© Copyright 2000 Dorsey Brothers Music Limited, 8/9 Frith Street, London W1.

All Rights Reserved. International Copyright Secured.

Var.2 **Minore**

Var.3 **Maggiore**

8

Allegro in B♭

(K3)

Composed by Wolfgang Amadeus Mozart

Moderately bright

© Copyright 2000 Dorsey Brothers Music Limited, 8/9 Frith Street, London W1.

All Rights Reserved. International Copyright Secured.

Allelujah

(from Exsultate, Jubilate)

Composed by Wolfgang Amadeus Mozart

© Copyright 2000 Dorsey Brothers Music Limited, 8/9 Frith Street, London W1.

All Rights Reserved. International Copyright Secured.

11

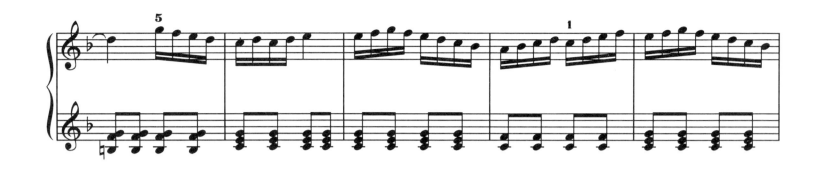

Ave Verum Corpus

(K618)

Composed by Wolfgang Amadeus Mozart

Not too slow

© Copyright 2000 Dorsey Brothers Music Limited, 8/9 Frith Street, London W1.

All Rights Reserved. International Copyright Secured.

15

Andante in E♭

Composed by Wolfgang Amadeus Mozart

© Copyright 2000 Dorsey Brothers Music Limited, 8/9 Frith Street, London W1.

All Rights Reserved. International Copyright Secured.

Clarinet Concerto

(K622 Slow Movement Theme)

Composed by Wolfgang Amadeus Mozart

© Copyright 2000 Dorsey Brothers Music Limited, 8/9 Frith Street, London W1.
All Rights Reserved. International Copyright Secured.

Contredanse

Composed by Wolfgang Amadeus Mozart

© Copyright 2000 Dorsey Brothers Music Limited, 8/9 Frith Street, London W1.

All Rights Reserved. International Copyright Secured.

Don't Be Shy

(from Così fan tutti K588)

Composed by Wolfgang Amadeus Mozart

Moderately

© Copyright 2000 Dorsey Brothers Music Limited, 8/9 Frith Street, London W1.
All Rights Reserved. International Copyright Secured.

Divertimento No.17

(K.334 Minuet)

Composed by Wolfgang Amadeus Mozart

© Copyright 2000 Dorsey Brothers Music Limited, 8/9 Frith Street, London W1.

All Rights Reserved. International Copyright Secured.

Drinking Song

(from Don Giovanni K527)

Composed by Wolfgang Amadeus Mozart

© Copyright 2000 Dorsey Brothers Music Limited, 8/9 Frith Street, London W1.
All Rights Reserved. International Copyright Secured.

Eine Kleine Nachtmusik

(K525 1st Movement Theme)

Composed by Wolfgang Amadeus Mozart

© Copyright 2000 Dorsey Brothers Music Limited, 8/9 Frith Street, London W1.
All Rights Reserved. International Copyright Secured.

Eine Kleine Nachtmusik

(K525 Minuetto)

Composed by Wolfgang Amadeus Mozart

With movement

© Copyright 2000 Dorsey Brothers Music Limited, 8/9 Frith Street, London W1.

All Rights Reserved. International Copyright Secured.

D.C. al fine

Eine Kleine Nachtmusik

(K525 Romance)

Composed by Wolfgang Amadeus Mozart

Slow

© Copyright 2000 Dorsey Brothers Music Limited, 8/9 Frith Street, London W1.
All Rights Reserved. International Copyright Secured.

Lacrymosa

(from Requiem K626)

Composed by Wolfgang Amadeus Mozart

© Copyright 2000 Dorsey Brothers Music Limited, 8/9 Frith Street, London W1.
All Rights Reserved. International Copyright Secured.

Lullaby

Composed by Wolfgang Amadeus Mozart

© Copyright 2000 Dorsey Brothers Music Limited, 8/9 Frith Street, London W1.
All Rights Reserved. International Copyright Secured.

Minuet in C

(K6)

Composed by Wolfgang Amadeus Mozart

Moderately

© Copyright 2000 Dorsey Brothers Music Limited, 8/9 Frith Street, London W1.
All Rights Reserved. International Copyright Secured.

Minuet in D

(K94)

Composed by Wolfgang Amadeus Mozart

© Copyright 2000 Dorsey Brothers Music Limited, 8/9 Frith Street, London W1.
All Rights Reserved. International Copyright Secured.

Minuet in F

(K2)

Composed by Wolfgang Amadeus Mozart

© Copyright 2000 Dorsey Brothers Music Limited, 8/9 Frith Street, London W1.

All Rights Reserved. International Copyright Secured.

O Isis And Osiris

(from The Magic Flute K620)

Composed by Wolfgang Amadeus Mozart

© Copyright 2000 Dorsey Brothers Music Limited, 8/9 Frith Street, London W1.
All Rights Reserved. International Copyright Secured.

Piano Concerto in C 'Elvira Madigan'

(K467 Theme)

Composed by Wolfgang Amadeus Mozart

© Copyright 2000 Dorsey Brothers Music Limited, 8/9 Frith Street, London W1.
All Rights Reserved. International Copyright Secured.

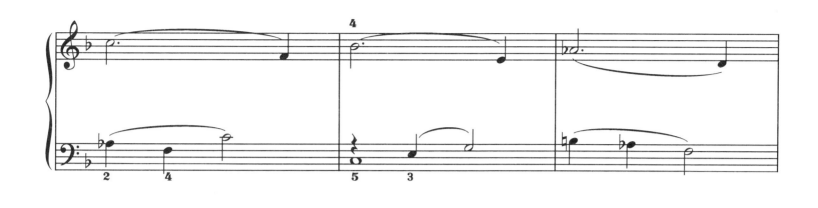

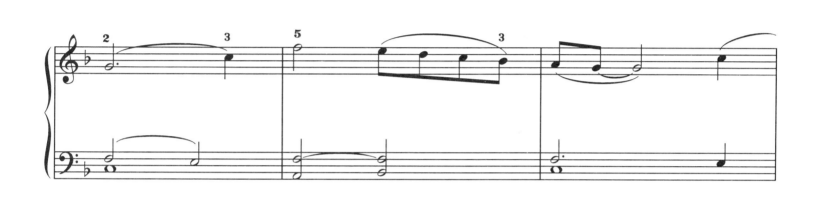

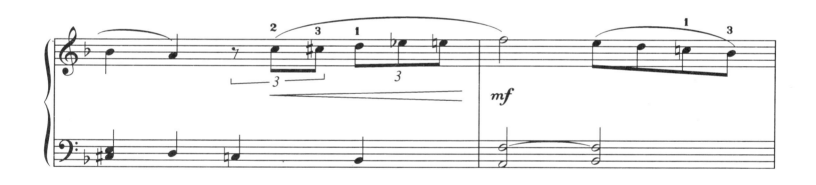

Piano Concerto in B♭

(K450 Slow Movement Theme)

Composed by Wolfgang Amadeus Mozart

© Copyright 2000 Dorsey Brothers Music Limited, 8/9 Frith Street, London W1.

All Rights Reserved. International Copyright Secured.

Piano Sonata in A

(K331 Andante Grazioso)

Composed by Wolfgang Amadeus Mozart

© Copyright 2000 Dorsey Brothers Music Limited, 8/9 Frith Street, London W1.
All Rights Reserved. International Copyright Secured.

Piano Sonata in A

(K331 Rondo alla Turka)

Composed by Wolfgang Amadeus Mozart

© Copyright 2000 Dorsey Brothers Music Limited, 8/9 Frith Street, London W1.
All Rights Reserved. International Copyright Secured.

Piano Sonata in B♭

(K570 Adagio)

Composed by Wolfgang Amadeus Mozart

© Copyright 2000 Dorsey Brothers Music Limited, 8/9 Frith Street, London W1.
All Rights Reserved. International Copyright Secured.

48

Piano Sonata in C

(K545 Allegro)

Composed by Wolfgang Amadeus Mozart

© Copyright 2000 Dorsey Brothers Music Limited, 8/9 Frith Street, London W1.

All Rights Reserved. International Copyright Secured.

The Manly Heart With Love O'erflowing

(from The Magic Flute K620)

Composed by Wolfgang Amadeus Mozart

© Copyright 2000 Dorsey Brothers Music Limited, 8/9 Frith Street, London W1.

All Rights Reserved. International Copyright Secured.

Say Goodbye Now To Pastime

(from The Marriage Of Figaro K492)

Composed by Wolfgang Amadeus Mozart

© Copyright 2000 Dorsey Brothers Music Limited, 8/9 Frith Street, London W1.
All Rights Reserved. International Copyright Secured.

Symphony No.35 'Haffner'

(K385 Minuetto Theme)

Composed by Wolfgang Amadeus Mozart

© Copyright 2000 Dorsey Brothers Music Limited, 8/9 Frith Street, London W1.
All Rights Reserved. International Copyright Secured.

Symphony No.39 in E♭

(K543 Minuet)

Composed by Wolfgang Amadeus Mozart

© Copyright 2000 Dorsey Brothers Music Limited, 8/9 Frith Street, London W1.
All Rights Reserved. International Copyright Secured.

Symphony No.40

(K550 1st Movement Theme)

Composed by Wolfgang Amadeus Mozart

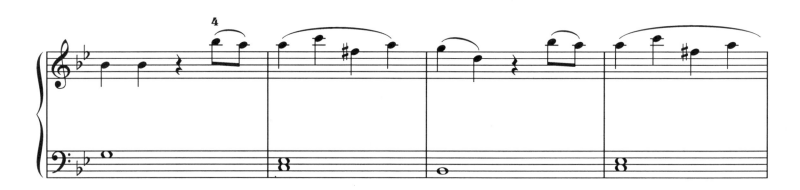

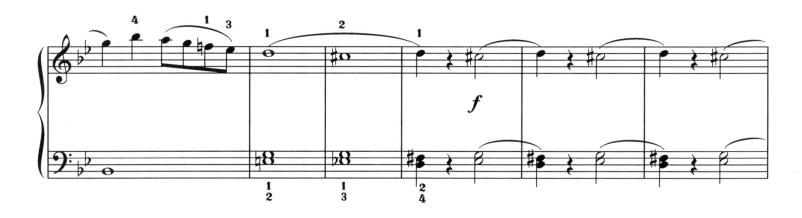

© Copyright 2000 Dorsey Brothers Music Limited, 8/9 Frith Street, London W1.

All Rights Reserved. International Copyright Secured.

Tell Me Fair Ladies

(from The Marriage Of Figaro K492)

Composed by Wolfgang Amadeus Mozart

Moderately

© Copyright 2000 Dorsey Brothers Music Limited, 8/9 Frith Street, London W1.

All Rights Reserved. International Copyright Secured.

Violin & Piano Sonata in C

(K296 Slow Movement Theme)

Composed by Wolfgang Amadeus Mozart

© Copyright 2000 Dorsey Brothers Music Limited, 8/9 Frith Street, London W1.
All Rights Reserved. International Copyright Secured.

Violin Concerto in D

(K211 Slow Movement Theme)

Composed by Wolfgang Amadeus Mozart

© Copyright 2000 Dorsey Brothers Music Limited, 8/9 Frith Street, London W1.

All Rights Reserved. International Copyright Secured.

Violin & Piano Sonata in E♭

(K481 Last Movement Theme)

Composed by Wolfgang Amadeus Mozart

© Copyright 2000 Dorsey Brothers Music Limited, 8/9 Frith Street, London W1.

All Rights Reserved. International Copyright Secured.

Zerlina's Song

(from Don Giovanni K527)

Composed by Wolfgang Amadeus Mozart

© Copyright 2000 Dorsey Brothers Music Limited, 8/9 Frith Street, London W1.
All Rights Reserved. International Copyright Secured.

Enjoy playing more *The Best of...* classics

Each book contains the composer's most popular works.
The series is a wonderful addition to your musical collection.

The Best of Bach
27 popular classics... choral works, movements
from orchestral suites and keyboard music, plus
a special biographical section on Bach. **Includes**
Air On The G String; Jesu, Joy Of Man's Desiring;
Prelude in C; Sheep May Safely Graze; and Toccata
& Fugue in D minor. 72pp. Order No. AM956637

The Best of Beethoven
28 famous classics... concertos, chamber music
and themes from symphonies, plus a special
biographical section on Beethoven. **Includes:**
Für Elise; 'Moonlight' Sonata (Theme); Ode To Joy
(from Symphony No.9) and 'Pathétique' Sonata
(2nd Movement Theme). 72pp. Order No. AM956626

Two great series designed for easy piano.

I Can Play That!...

Bach - 21 pieces.
Order No. AM91041

Mozart - 25 pieces.
Order No. AM91043

Beethoven - 17 pieces.
Order No. AM91042

Operatic Arias - 21 pieces.
Order No. AM91312

Classics - 22 pieces.
Order No. AM89927

Popular Classics - 24 pieces.
Order No. AM952611

Handel - 20 pieces.
Order No. AM91299

Symphonic Themes -
20 pieces. 48pp.
Order No. AM91313

It's Easy To Play...

Bach - 21pieces. 48pp.
Order No. AM71721

Classics - 25 pieces. 48pp.
Order No. AM19563

Schubert - 20 pieces. 48pp.
Order No. AM71762

Ballet Music - 11 pieces. 48pp.
Order No. AM32939

Classics 2 - 23 pieces. 48pp.
Order No. AM60252

Strauss - 11 pieces. 48pp.
Order No. AM83791

Beethoven - 20 pieces. 48pp.
Order No. AM71739

Mozart - 20 pieces. 48pp.
Order No. AM71754

Tchaikovsky - 14 pieces. 48pp.
Order No. AM82926

Chopin - 24 pieces. 48pp.
Order No. AM71747

Opera - 15 pieces. 48pp.
Order No. AM32152

Popular Classics - 25 pieces.
48pp. Order No. AM952490

Classical Themes - 21pieces.
48pp. Order No. AM31659

Available from all good music retailers or, in case of difficulty,
contact Music Sales Limited, Sales & Distribution Centre,
Newmarket Road, Bury St. Edmunds, Suffolk IP33 3YP.
Telephone 01284 725725; Fax 01284 702592.

See also page 2 for details of Music Sales' complete
colour catalogues!

www.musicsales.com